R.W. Younkin

Is Death the End?

THE CHRISTIAN ANSWER

CARROLL E. SIMCOX

Greenwich · Connecticut

1959

303-859-C-4
© 1959 by The Seabury Press, Incorporated
Library of Congress Catalog Card Number: 59-9963
Printed in the United States of America

This book is written in loving memory of William, George, Jessie, and some others known to the author and well known to God, of whom the Spirit says:

Blessed are the dead which die in the Lord from henceforth: . . . that they may rest from their labors; and their works do follow them.

Revelation 14:13

Preface

As a teacher of Christianity, I can testify that there are few subjects which evoke more questions from all sorts and conditions of people than does the Christian doctrine of eternal life. This book is an attempt to set forth that doctrine as simply as I can. The reader should not expect to find here any strictly new light upon the mysteries of life, death, and the life to come; for the only real light we have is that which Jesus Christ has shed upon it. Yet the "old" light has a strange way of becoming "new" to us whenever we sit down and think about these ultimate things in the presence of our Lord and under the guidance of His Spirit.

At the moment of this writing, the holy Church throughout all the world is celebrating Christ's Easter Victory, by which death is conquered for us. That victory is the assurance that our hope of glory is not in vain. Because He lives, we shall live also.

CARROLL E. SIMCOX

Eastertide, 1959

Contents

1

The Arch Fear

ONE DAY, some thirteen hundred years ago, some of our British ancestors were gathered in the court of King Edward of Northumbria. They had something unusual and momentous to talk about. They were pagans, and some Christian missionaries had just arrived in the realm. The question was: "Shall we give them a hearing?" They had their own ancestral religion, and these Christians had come to win them to another faith if they could. At length a grim old warrior stood up and asked: "Can this new religion tell us of what happens after death? The life of man is like a swallow flying through this lighted hall. It enters in at one door from the darkness outside, and flitting through the light and warmth passes through the farther door into the dark unknown beyond. Can this new religion solve for us the mystery? What comes to men in the dark, dim unknown?"

It is a matter of history that the Christian missionaries succeeded. Evidently they gave to those Britons a satisfying answer.

Our subject in this book is that Christian answer to man's indomitable question, as Job expresses it: "If a man die, shall he live again?" (*Job 14:14*)

8 ॐ

We say that the Christian missionaries gave the Britons "the answer." Before going any farther, we had better state exactly what we mean by "the answer." When we say of somebody that "he knows all the answers," we are attributing to him an omniscience which, of course, he cannot possibly have on any subject at all. Albert Einstein knew more of "the answers" about mathematics and physics than most, but if he had ever heard you say that he knew all the answers he would have corrected you most emphatically. Nobody knows all the answers about the simplest thing. Everybody walks by faith rather than by full sight about anything. The old British chieftain wanted to know what comes to men in the dark, dim unknown beyond the grave; and he wanted to know exactly and completely what it is. So do we. The Christian missionaries couldn't give him that knowledge, because it was not theirs to give. They didn't know all the answers. What they had to give was a knowledge of God which is a great deal better than all the answers.

We are approaching our subject with this understanding. We shall pay little attention to the so-called arguments for immortality—and there are some good ones. Our reason for this is that we are thinking religiously rather than philosophically. Let me explain this distinction. The philosopher tries to answer Job's question by reasoning about the nature of man. His main question is: Is there an imperishable something in man, call it soul or personality or whatever you will, which by its very nature survives death? The religionist, if he is a Christian, starts with God rather than with man. His question is: What do we know about God, and about God's will and purpose for man? The answer to that question will answer the question: If a man die, shall he live again? We are following this religious line of reasoning in this book.

One further word about the philosophical arguments for immortality. The truth about them is as Dr. Paul Tillich expresses it:

"The anxiety of fate and death is most basic, most universal, and inescapable. All attempts to argue it away are futile. Even if the so-called arguments for the 'immortality of the soul' had argumentative power (which they do not have) they would not convince existentially. For existentially everybody is aware of the complete loss of self which biological extinction implies." [1]

By "existentially" Tillich means humanly. Our haunting anxiety about our death is a simple human fact. If these arguments for our immortality were overwhelmingly convincing, that anxiety would still be there. Convince a man beyond all shadow of doubt that he has an immortal soul; none the less he will say: "But I must still die; and this biological extinction of death annihilates my self. My soul may live on; but my soul isn't the whole, complete *I*. What becomes of *me?*"

If the man is persuaded that he is a child of God's love, and if he has a child of his own whom he wishes he could keep to himself forever, he is on the way to a satisfying conviction on this subject of his post-mortem destiny. But this, you see, is a religious faith, not a philosophical opinion.

When we say that we are thinking religiously rather than philosophically we certainly do not mean that we are not really thinking. Christians should never let themselves forget for a moment the divine commandment to love God with all their heart and soul and *mind*. To love God with all your mind is to think as well and as hard as you can about truth as God shows it to you. God doesn't do our thinking for us. He shows us some glimpse of His will and His ways and He says to us: "Now *think* about it. Use the brains I have given you."

This we shall stedfastly try to do, God helping us.

Our thinking will be primarily about God, and only secondarily about man, since it is in the character of God as we know Him, rather than in our own human being, that we look for our answer to the great question. Yet we must begin with a question about man. Does man desire immortality? Or, to put it another way, does man fear death? Is our desire for immortality one of those hungers which belong to our very nature, such as the hunger for food or for sex or for beauty? This is an important question, because this seems to be a world in which every really basic appetite of man is meant to have a possible fulfillment. There is food enough on our planet to satisfy everybody's bodily hunger, if we all work hard and plan sensibly. The existence of such an elemental desire in man suggests that it is meant to be satisfied. Does man radically fear death as extinction? Does man radically hunger for life beyond death?

Browning begins his *Prospice* with these lines:

Fear death?—to feel the fog in my throat,
   The mist in my face,
When the snows begin, and the blasts denote
   I am nearing the place,
The power of the night, the press of the storm,
   The post of the foe;
Where he stands, the Arch Fear in a visible form . . .

The Arch Fear—the fear of all fears: is this what death means to us? Offhand and casually we may answer no. "I expect to die," one says, "and I try to live in daily preparedness for it; I hope I can put it off for a good long while, but I'm not afraid of it." Such a reply may be as honest as it is brave, but the person who makes it may not know himself nearly as thoroughly as he thinks he does. The whole truth about himself is, as Tillich says, that "the anxiety of death is most basic, most universal, and most inescapable." We are not always conscious of this anxiety in ourselves, but it is in us none the less. If we do not fear death, why do we fight it so resolutely? The whole of our medical science is one vast conspiracy to cheat the undertaker. H. G. Wells truly remarked that "people can go through life fudging, evading and sidestepping till their first contact with elemental realities in the cold sweat of their deathbed." It is not so, apparently, with the dog or the sheep. When the animal's instinct tells it that its time to die has come, it will seek out a quiet spot, lie down and die without any mental anguish. But man's whole natural life may be fairly described as one long and constant effort to evade and to post-pone the inevitable hour. This anxiety that we may sink from being into non-being is as basic as anything in us.

The absence of this anxiety from any individual is so abnormal that the rest of us regard it as insanity. We consider that a person with a bent toward suicide, or even one who is indifferent to whether he lives or dies, cannot be in his right mind. The existence of the anxiety of death is a mark of sanity. Assuming that we are creatures of God, we may here note the significant fact that God puts this anxiety in us, or at least that He allows it to be in us.

Now, this anxiety is a symptom of something else. It bears witness to man's primal hunger for a life that runs beyond death. If our very nature told us that death is the end of our being, we should accept it as casually as the dog accepts it. But our nature seems to tell us something else—hence our anxiety. It seems to tell us that it is *not fitting* that we should perish as the beasts of the field. Yet we seem to; and our anxiety of death is the psychic sign of this conflict between what seems unfitting and what seems to be our fate.

Concerning this, another great Victorian poet clothes our thoughts in words. In Tennyson's familiar verses written in mournful memory of his friend Edward Hallam we read this apostrophe to God:

> Thou wilt not leave us in the dust:
>   Thou madest man, he knows not why;
> He thinks he was not made to die;
>   And thou hast made him: thou art just.

Indubitably man thinks he was not made to die, and this is why he resists death so strenuously. If he believes in God, he appeals his case to God. "Thou madest man, he knows not why." Man does know, however, that

God in making him has endowed him with this hunger for more life. It must be for something. Every one of our other radical hungers is for something, and God provides that every other hunger shall be satisfied. Is this hunger for immortality the one exception—a cruel trick of our Maker, like holding out to a man tormented with thirst a glass of ice water and then pulling it away from him? "Thou hast made him: thou art just." We hope so.

There is, of course, another interpretation that can be given to our anxiety of death and our desire to postpone our death for as long as possible. Mr. Wells and many others have argued that it is selfish and egotistical for a man to want to live forever; who is he to suppose that he is so "all-fired important" in the cosmic scheme of things? It must be conceded that a person may well desire his own immortality thus selfishly and egotistically, but it can hardly be maintained that this egotistical self-regard is the only, or even the primary, motivation of this anxiety of death and hunger for life as a basic human fact. The man in a torment of thirst wants water, not because he is selfish but because his nature shrieks that he ought to have it. So with this hunger for life in face of death. A less selfish and egotistical person than Sir Wildred Grenfell, the great Labrador doctor, could hardly be found among all the communion of saints. He once remarked: "As for the life after death, I know nothing about it; but I want it, whatever it is." A man like Grenfell wants the life everlasting because his experience of the present life is such as to make him realize that he can do no more on this earth than make a fair beginning of life as it is meant to be.

The poet William Cowper was another of those who have made just enough of this life to realize how much more they need for real self-fulfilment. His friendship with Lady Hesketh was the kind of noble union of minds and spirits which raises human life to its highest level of meaning and worth. He once wrote to her: "You must know that I should not love you half so well, if I did not believe you would be my friend to eternity. There is not room enough for friendship to unfold itself in such a nook of life as this."

From this kind of testimony we draw one conclusion: that when people live as God wants them to live, to His glory and to the benefit of their fellow men, God whets their appetites for more life than their brief mortal span and their cramping earthly limitations can possibly contain. Their desire for immortality is itself an intimation of immortality, given to them by God Himself, if we agree with Tennyson in believing that "God is just." A just Creator will not give us a hunger that is all for nothing.

2

Intimations of Immortality

WE HAVE laid it down as our working principle that we must seek in God Himself, in His manifested will and purpose for His human creatures, our answer to the question, "If a man die, shall he live again?" This does not mean, however, that whatever we find in man as man is irrelevant to our quest. For God has made man with all that is in him; whatever we find in man, sin excepted, is put there by God. A fear of death, a desire for immortality, is a part of man's essential being, and it is therefore the work of God. If man has any intimations of his own immortality, these are the work of the almighty hand that made him.

For the Christian, the decisive reason for believing in immortality is the promise of Jesus Christ, who says to us: "Because I live, ye shall live also." (*St. John 14:19*) Christ's power to make good His promise to us is triumphantly vindicated by His resurrection from the dead. This we shall thoroughly consider later on. For the present, let us try to assume that we have never heard of Christ, and let us consider those intimations of immortality which are given to man entirely independently of the revelation of Christ.

The most natural approach is historical. To try to survey all of the great pre-Christian cultures and religions with their expressions of man's deathless hope would take us far beyond the scope of a small book, so we shall limit our view to those two pre-Christian traditions which have influenced most directly our own inheritance—the Greek and the Hebrew.

Both Greek and Hebrew took for granted that man survives death in some form and degree. However differently their thought processes worked, they came to this same conclusion. The critic may glibly explain it as "wishful thinking," but if there was anything that moved either Greek or Hebrew to believe in life beyond death it was certainly not this, for the kind of postmortem existence they envisaged was anything but blissful. Roughly speaking, the Greek and the Hebrew, during their classic eras from the ninth to the fourth centuries B.C., held substantially the same view of the after life. It was not an attractive prospect. The Greek called it Hades and the Hebrew called it Sheol; in either case it was pretty nearly what we call hell. In the eleventh book of the Odyssey, Odysseus is given an audience with some of his departed comrades now in the gloomy house of Hades. When the shade of Achilles appears before him, Odysseus says: "When you were on earth, in the old days, we Argives honored you as though you were a god; and now, down here, you are a mighty prince among the dead. For you, Achilles, Death should have lost his sting." To this Achilles replies: "My lord Odysseus, spare me your praise of death. Put me on earth again, and I would rather be a serf in the house of some landless man, with little enough for himself to live on, than king of all these dead men that have done with life." Such was the dominant Greek view of the life of Hades: not real life, but barren and hopeless existence. The Hebrew view which permeates almost all of the Old Testament is very similar. Hezekiah, King of Judah, staring death in the face, laments to God: "The grave (Sheol) cannot praise thee, death cannot celebrate thee: they that go down into the pit cannot hope for thy truth. The living, the living, he shall praise thee as I do this day." (*Isaiah 38:18-19*) "The living" are those who have not yet died; they who have died miserably exist in Sheol, beyond the reach of God's goodness.

So there is a basic similarity in the Greek and Hebrew ideas of the after life. But there is an important difference in their respective ways of thinking about human destiny. The Greek was inclined to think of "the divine in man." The Jew never did that. If there is something divine in man, and this divine element is immortal in itself, it follows that at least this divine part of man survives death. Hebrew thought, on the contrary, kept ever in mind the great gulf fixed between God and man: they are totally different beings. This is the chief difference between the two traditions, and it is profoundly momentous in its consequences. It means that the Hebrew moves toward a view that places man's fate and destiny entirely in the hands of God, while the Greek moves toward the view that man is immortal simply because he is man, and immortality belongs to human nature as such. Yet, beneath these differences of approach, is to be found a common intimation of immortality—this feeling that man is not born to die utterly and completely.

But was all this just a vague feeling, with no real reasoning behind it? The suggestion is incredible to anybody who has any knowledge of the ancient Greeks and Hebrews. They were thinkers. Their reasoning about this came out of this simple observable fact about a dead man: that something has passed from him, leaving only this lifeless corpse which once was his body. The corpse is observably dead. But that extra something— the life, the soul, *psyche* (Greek), or *nephesh* (Hebrew), is not observably dead; it is simply gone. Whither? Into what condition? Hades-Sheol is the answer. We cannot know anything directly about this mysterious realm or condition; we can only guess about it, and mythologize.

There is an interesting Latin verse, beginning *Animala blandula vagula* and traditionally supposed to be the Roman Emperor Hadrian's alloquy to his soul, which runs something like this:

> Odd little comrade, comfortable guest,
> Capricious, elfin puff of air,
> You're off: but where?
> And when you've left this breast,
> Tense little traveler, pale and bare,
> Will you find anything to laugh at there?

It expresses this deep-rooted belief about that extra something in man that goes forth at death to some mysterious new estate, and it expresses the pathetic anxiety man is bound to feel as he tries to conceive of his soul separated from the body. "Will you find anything to laugh at there?" Can life be happy and whole, warm-blooded and truly alive, to the disembodied soul? One must fear not; hence the gloom of Hades-Sheol in general belief. But the significant point about the belief for our present purpose is its witness to the deep and almost universal conviction that man is more than the body that dies. It is a real intimation of immortality, and we may reasonably believe that God gives it to man as a part of man's necessary knowledge of himself.

We turn now to another ancient, widespread, and persistent intimation of immortality, which we may call the moral argument for immortality.

Once man has risen above the brute level, he finds himself with a conscience, a sense that he ought to do some things and that he ought not to do some other things. Many modern sociologists are quick to explain that this is all the result of society's education of the individual. A society finds that it cannot hold together unless it can train its members to abstain from murder, theft, adultery, treason, and other socially destructive acts, and this is self-evidently true. But if we infer from this that the individual's conscience, his sense of ought-ness, is given to him entirely by his human society we are not covering the whole ground that needs to be explained. For the most characteristic quality of private conscience is its sense of accountability, not simply to one's human judges, but to whatever gods may be. The typical man, whether of Solon's Athens or of Isaiah's Jerusalem or of Villon's Paris or of Sinclair Lewis' Main Street, does not behave as he does simply and solely because he covets the rewards and fears the punishment of his community. However he expresses it, however dimly he feels it, he considers himself accountable to the universe itself for his behavior. He feels that the stars in their courses are on the side of right and against wrong. (That men's particular ideas of what is right or wrong widely differ is not to the present point.) When Stevenson said that he believed in "an ultimate decency of things" he spoke for the human race as a whole.

The almost universal consensus is that we live in a world in which the good is ultimately rewarded and the evil is ultimately punished. But once men reach this conclusion they encounter a scandalous fact, which is this: that the righteous man does not always get his just reward in this present life, nor does the wicked man always get his just punishment. Nothing could be plainer. If the ultimate decency of things is to be finally vindicated in every man's life, it can only be in some extension, some dimension, of life beyond this mortal range. On this logic, immortality becomes a necessity.

It must be granted that all this is entirely hypothetical. *If* there is an ultimate decency of things, and *if* it is true that final justice is never done to the individual in this present life, then it follows that the final justice will be done in a life after death. But the second of these two *if* propositions seems practically incontestable. Socrates drinking the hemlock—Christ on His cross—the wicked man prospering as the green bay tree: these are grievously familiar spectacles. As for the first proposition, the Grand Perhaps that there is an ultimate decency of things, most of the wisest minds and noblest spirits of all ages have believed it, and the common man has been with them. Most would say that life makes no sense on any other hypothesis. Therefore we have a very solid right of reason to call it an intimation (not a proof) of immortality.

There is one more idea and feeling which has a deep hold on a large part of the human race and which we may take as an intimation or hint of immortality. (Please note once again that I am not calling these "intimations" proofs or even arguments. I say no more than that they may be leadings, given to us by God.) This idea is man's conviction that he has within himself possibilities of development and fruition which can never be fulfilled in threescore years and ten, or even fourscore and ten. Not every man has this idea. If a person lives a very grubby life of animal contentment, satisfied with his plenty of food and drink and friends and fun and asking no more, he will not have this hunger for more life. One world is enough for him. But this philosophy has never been able to satisfy the better specimens of our race.

It was said of Stevenson that he died with a thousand stories in his heart. Life was far too short for him to exhaust his creative impulse. This is true of everybody who lives by the impulse to create, to do, to give. No matter how long he lives, he can never go to his grave content that he has done his work.

Does God give us this driving desire to "give everything we've got" to our work, then deny to us the time and the scope we need for doing it? If death is the end of all our being and doing, this must be our conclusion. In that case, God manages His world rather badly. He makes creatures who are only beginning to do their best work for Him when He kills them off . . . unless there is more to come.

In the following chapters we shall consider the Christian answer, in which, Christians believe, these intimations of immortality are vindicated and validated and enlightened by the great Light of God Himself focussed upon the dark gloom and somber mystery of the grave.

3

Christ's Teaching

WE COME now to the main subject of this book, the Christian doctrine of life beyond death, a subject which we deliberately avoided in the last chapter as we considered the ideas, hopes and fears which seem to be found in all men alike.

Christianity is different from all other religions—radically and fundamentally different; and this differentness is nowhere more emphatic than in this area of belief about the life to come. What makes the difference is that in the Christian faith there is *a resurrection already done*. No other religion makes any such claim. Indeed, no other religion claims for its founder or saviour or leader what Christians claim concerning their Lord in such terms as these:

"And [I believe] in Jesus Christ, his only Son our Lord: Who was conceived by the Holy Ghost, Born of the Virgin Mary: Suffered under Pontius Pilate, Was crucified, dead, and buried: He descended into hell; The third day he rose again from the dead: He ascended into heaven, And sitteth on the right hand of God the Father Almighty: From thence he shall come to judge the quick and the dead."

The moment we stop to think what we are saying in these tremendous affirmations we realize that we are making a colossal claim about somebody who lived many ages ago and about whom we have very little historical information. How do we know all this about Him? How can we prove it? Well, we can't prove it, in the sense of demonstrating beyond all reasonable doubt that He was what we think He was. But Christians believe it because they believe that Christ is alive right now; and they believe He is alive right now because they have dealings with Him. He was once dead. Nobody questions that. But He did not stay dead, obviously, if it is possible for Him to have actual communication with us today. The crucial claim is that Christ is risen from the dead. If we are convinced of this, the other claims about Him—that He was the Son of God, that He worked miracles, that He can save us from death—all fall into place naturally enough. We believe in Christ and we believe what He tells us about God's will and plans for us because we believe that He Himself is risen from the dead and is now and forever alive.

The Gospels record for us numerous teachings of Jesus concerning the life to come, although we must take careful note of the fact that He did not preach and teach a strictly other-worldly religion. Many of our traditional ideas of heaven and hell, which are commonly called Christian, do not come from Him. This is as good a place as any to get it clear in our minds what Jesus did *not* teach about the life to come. Some of these conventional ideas are very childish, and worse, but all too many people suppose that they are Christian.

One of these ideas is that when an acceptably good person dies he becomes an angel in heaven. This flatly contradicts the Bible, which consistently maintains that angels and men are beings in totally different orders. A man when he enters into the life to come remains a man.

Another conventional idea with no warrant of the Gospel suggests that in heaven we shall have nothing to do except—as an old hymn expresses it—"to gaze and gaze on God." Jesus teaches that the life of heaven is a life of perfect fellowship with God, but such fellowship implies a sharing in God's own work.

Then there is the idea that the joy of heaven will consist of getting whatever we want, when we want it, and all that we want. The plain teaching of Jesus is that we shall not enter the heavenly kingdom until we want only what God wants—a very different thing.

It is perhaps needless to say that Jesus gives no support whatever for any belief that unbaptized persons are cast into hell for being unbaptized. Yet there are many who suppose that this is the orthodox Christian doctrine.

The whole conception of hell as a place in which the damned are subjected to fiendish torments by the will of the God whose majesty they have offended and who is thus getting even with them is a monstrous slander against God, and it is inconceivable how anybody can read the Gospels and suppose that this is Christian doctrine. Yet the world around us still seems to think that if we take the words of Jesus seriously we are committed to such a belief.

I have mentioned a few of the more familiar parodies

and distortions of the Christian doctrine, with some additions to it; there are others which are equally false. It will help us to detect such errors if we fix in mind what Jesus positively does teach about our eternal destiny, and to that we now turn.

Jesus does not give us a formal and systematic doctrine of the life to come, telling us precisely what heaven is like, what hell is like, who goes to one place and who to the other. There is the best of reasons for this. It is that we could not understand Him if He did. We are in no condition at present to conceive realistically the nature of a life which is as far beyond our present experience as the life of a saint and sage of eighty is beyond the life of a fetus of three months. What Jesus gives us, in His teaching and still more in His personal revelation of God to us, is a knowledge of God which makes us certain that "the best is yet to be" for him who loves God. He assures us that we are in God's hands, in death as in life, and that God is an all-just Judge and an all-loving Father.

The parables and sayings of Jesus which touch at all upon the life to come are hints and suggestions to guide us on our way toward that glory which shall be revealed when we are ready for it—after we have passed into that dimension of life which we call eternity.

Some of these pronouncements of Jesus we shall now examine, to get the most important data in our minds.

We must begin with a very general statement. The central proclamation of Christ's Gospel is the kingdom of God: its coming, its presence, its power and glory, its openness to all believers in Him. If men will take Christ at His word and let Him reconcile them to their Father, if they will take upon themselves the yoke of obedience of Him, they will enter the kingdom; and because the kingdom is an everlasting kingdom they shall abide in its joy forever. The kingdom of God is the realized rule of God in human life. Where God's will is done, there is the kingdom—on earth as it is in heaven. To enter this kingdom, to come under God's rule as God's obedient child, is to enter into a life in which death is swallowed up in victory. Conversely, to reject the kingdom when it is opened to one is to remain in the outer darkness, and some of Christ's more somber sayings warn us that this can be forever. Throughout His teachings Jesus assumes the everlastingness of human life. He admits no possibility that a person can escape from life by dying. One can die to God, but one cannot die to life; and life, here or hereafter, is either in the kingdom of God or out of it.

The many parables of the kingdom and other utterances of Jesus which have any bearing upon man's eternal destiny are all commentaries upon the principle which we have just summarized.

Let us look now at some of the parables of Jesus which are specially relevant to our subject.

St. Luke records for us (*12:16-21*) Christ's parable of the rich fool who was so busy building new and bigger barns that he neglected his soul. Then one day God told him that he must die that night. What had he to take with him into eternity? His money? "You can't take it with you." The one thing you can and must take with you is your own self, with which you must live forever. The story powerfully suggests that what we shall be forever we are now becoming, for better or for worse.

The parable of the great supper (*St. Luke 14:15-24*) tells how the people who got the gilt-edged invitations made light of their friend's hospitality and how the host then invited all sorts of riff-raff to come to his splendid banquet. It means, among other things, that if we reach heaven we shall be surprised to see some of the "strange characters" who are God's honored guests.

The wonderful stories of the lost sheep, the lost coin, and the lost boy in St. Luke's fifteenth chapter reveal God's inexhaustible love and indefatigable searching for each individual soul. Nobody needs to despair of final acceptance by God so long as he knows that God not only holds open for him the door of the Father's house but will follow him to the ends of the earth to recover him. Jesus makes it clear in many other sayings, however, that we are not to presume upon God's love and patience as if to say: "Whatever I do now, God will forgive me and take me in when the time comes: He's that way."

The story of the rich man and Lazarus (*St. Luke 16:19-31*) is one of our Lord's most vivid and moving parables, and many have taken its picturesque details as concrete information about heaven and hell. This is a mistake. Christ's purpose in telling it is not to give us a map of the world to come but to warn us of two things: first, that the time to make our lives fit for heaven is now—with no time to lose; and second, that if we neglect compassion toward our fellow men we reject God's compassion for us and we doom ourselves to rejection from heaven.

In the parable of the workers in the vineyard (*St. Matthew 20:1-16*) Jesus teaches that only God can judge of the rewards He will give to His servants. We cannot earn heaven by our own exertions, and we are in no position to judge of what God should give to one or withhold from another.

The parable which has probably had the most influence upon Christian thinking about the last judgment is the parable of the sheep and the goats. (*St. Matthew 25:31-46*) Here is very definite teaching as to the principle of judgment by which we are finally pronounced acceptable or unacceptable to God for all eternity. That principle is our reaction to Christ as we meet Him in the persons of "the least of these" His brethren—the hungry, the thirsty, the stranger, the naked, the sick, the prisoner. We cannot love and serve Christ except as we love and serve Him in our fellow men. He is "in" them in such a way that whatever we do to anybody we do to Him; and at the final testing of our lives for their fitness for eternal fellowship with Christ this will be the test. In His summation of the meaning, at the end of the parable, Christ says that those who fail to meet this test will go into eternal punishment, while those whose life on earth has met this test will go into eternal life.

Let us note, before passing from the parables, these specially important points which are implied and asserted by them: first, that Christ Himself is the judge who pronounces the verdict as to what our eternal destiny is; second, that there are both heaven and hell; and third, that it is our present life on earth which determines our destiny, and the basis of that determination is our reaction to Christ.

We may now examine a few of His sayings which are not in parable form.

In the Sermon on the Mount we find this pronouncement: "If thy right eye offend thee, pluck it out, and cast it from thee: for it is profitable for thee that one of thy members should perish, and not that thy whole body should be cast into hell." (*St. Matthew 5:29*) This implies that a human life is an indivisible unit in the sight of God, and that the whole man, as a whole, is accepted for heaven or cast into hell. It is futile to hope that we shall be judged solely by the good that is in us—if there is any. Everything in us must be made ready for heaven.

The familiar words (*St. Matthew 6:19-20*) about laying up treasure in heaven, where neither moth nor rust consume, instruct us that the only treasures worth cultivating are those treasures of personal character which we can take with us into eternity and keep forever.

Christ's saying (*St. Matthew 7:13-14*) about the narrow gate and the strait way which lead to life are a warning that we cannot simply coast to heaven—we must climb. The work of preparing for heaven is necessarily a hard struggle for anybody. There is no easy salvation.

Jesus shared with most of His countrymen of His day the belief in a general resurrection, and in one of His exchanges with His critics He gives us some important instruction on the nature of the life to some. (See

St. Matthew 22:23-33, St. Mark 12:18-27, or *St. Luke 20:27-38*) The Sadducees, who denied that there is any resurrection, posed to Him the question: If a man has seven wives in succession before dying, which of them will be his wife in the life to come? Jesus replied that "they that are accounted worthy to attain to that world, and the resurrection from the dead, neither marry, nor are given in marriage; for neither can they die any more: for they are equal unto the angels; and are sons of God, being sons of the resurrection." (*St. Luke 20:35-36*) This may not tell us very much positively about the life to come, but it does suggest that in that life our present earthly relationships are transmuted, and in a sense transcended, in a new and higher life of love which is beyond our present understanding.

All Christians know and love Christ's wonderful assurance expressed by St. John: "In my Father's house are many mansions: if it were not so, I would have told you. I go to prepare a place for you." (*St. John 14:2*) The Greek word here translated "mansions" really means "resting-places," of the sort that weary travelers find along a caravan route. The suggestion is that in eternity we find places of rest and refreshment on our journey toward the Father. In the life to come there is opportunity for further growth and development in the direction of perfect Christ-likeness.

We may consider one more pre-resurrection saying of Jesus—His word to the penitent thief on the cross (*St. Luke 23:39-43*). This malefactor realized his own guilt, and appealed to Jesus: "Lord, remember me when thou comest into thy kingdom." Jesus answers him with the assurance of one who has no doubt that He is in a position to speak as Lord of the coming kingdom: "Verily I say unto thee, Today shalt thou be with me in paradise." He does not say "heaven." He seems to imply quite clearly that "paradise" is an experience of preparation for heaven—as it were, the vestibule of heaven. This man laden with sin is not ready for the perfected life of heaven, which is perfect union of will and harmony of character with Christ the Lord of heaven. But because he puts his whole trust in Jesus to receive him as His own, he is accepted and he is assured that heaven will be his final goal—by way of the preparation and purification of paradise.

All that we have considered in this chapter of the teachings of Jesus would have to be regarded as mere theory and speculation by one man, who might well be mistaken, were it not for one thing: He died, as all men must die, and then He rose again from the dead. This makes Christians bold to believe that He knew what He was talking about.

4

Christ's Resurrection

B UT DID Jesus rise from the dead? How can we be sure? It is foolish to try to brush off or to by-pass the question. The world wants with all its heart to believe this good news from the grave, but it dares not deceive itself about so important a matter as this and it demands to know what basis there is for believing that Jesus Christ has conquered death—for Himself and for all men.

The world asks for *proof*. And before we go any further we must take a close look at what we mean by proving something to be true. In our scientific age we are familiar with a type of proving scientific theories which is most admirable and impressive. A medical researcher may believe that he has discovered a drug which will kill the germs which produce the common cold. He inoculates thousands of white rats with his drug, and if the results are favorable he tries it on several thousand human beings. If the incidence of colds among these people over a year's time is much lower than the average, we say that he has proved his point.

Some propositions can be proved in this way, but many others cannot. It should be quite clear that no event alleged to have occurred in the past can be proved in any such way. There is no laboratory proof of the assertion that Washington crossed the Delaware or that Shakespeare wrote the plays of Shakespeare. A man can never prove by a laboratory demonstration that his wife is true to him. A child can never prove in this way that his mother loves him. And the Christian apologist can never prove in this way that Christ was crucified, dead, and buried, and that on the third day He rose from the dead; for that matter, he cannot prove in this way even that Christ actually lived.

It should be clear enough by now that every reasonable person goes through life believing all sorts of things that can never be "proved" in that one particular way of laboratory demonstration. So it would be a very narrow and stupid intellectual bigotry to say that we can reasonably believe only that which can be demonstrated in the way that our medical researcher has demonstrated the validity of his theory.

The resurrection of Christ took place as an event in history, if it did take place; and it must be examined in the way that alleged historical events are investigated. It is said that William the Norman successfully invaded England in 1066. How can we test the truth of this assertion? There are two lines of inquiry open to us. First, we can read and study the reports of the event which have come down to us from people who saw it happen. And second, we can consider the consequences of the event. Before William's conquest, England was entirely Anglo-Saxon in its politics and culture. After William's conquest it was profoundly changed. Something revolutionary happened. We know of nothing else that could have brought about so radical a change in England. All things considered, both the eyewitness accounts and the nature of the consequences, we conclude that William conquered England in 1066. Our accounts of the event may be confusing and contradictory in their details. We may not be sure at just what hour of the morning the battle of Hastings began, or just how many troops there were on each side; but the event itself seems to be established beyond all reasonable doubt.

The Christian reasoning about the alleged event of Christ's rising alive from the dead follows this general line. There were witnesses and there were consequences.

The witnesses of the resurrection would be those who claimed to have seen Jesus alive after His death. It is not claimed that any human eye saw the event in its actual happening—the dead body coming to life.

The earliest reference in the New Testament, in time of writing, is not to be found in any of the four Gospels but in St. Paul's first letter to the Corinthians, which was written about A.D. 55. His testimony reads: "I handed on to you in the beginning the message which I had received: namely, that Christ died for us sinners, as the Scriptures declared that He should, and was buried, and that on the third day He was raised to life again, in accordance with the Scriptures; and that He was seen by Cephas, then by the twelve, and then by more than five hundred brethren all at one time, of whom most are still alive but some have died. Then He was seen by James, then by all the apostles; and last of all He was seen by me, as one born out of due time." (*I Corinthians 15:3-9*)

Paul makes it clear that this was the Gospel as he had received it, and it is clear that all Christians agree that this was the great Christian claim. He writes well within the lifetime of many who were among the original witnesses. Paul is saying: If anyone is skeptical, let him talk to as many of those witnesses as he wishes; there are plenty of them.

Let us note first that the number of people who claimed to have seen Christ alive after His death is impressively large. It runs to hundreds. But what of their reliability? Were they truthful? Were they sane? So long as we are trying to be strictly impartial, we must face the question squarely and without prejudice.

It is conceivable that hundreds of people might get together on a story which is pure story and pure fiction in the interest of some common end. But we know well what the hostile world did to these witnesses. They were fiercely and cruelly persecuted; outlawed, slandered, imprisoned, tortured, and done to death. Yet they stubbornly stuck to their tale. There is only one reasonable conclusion: they believed their own story. This was no consciously fabricated lie.

There remains the question of their sanity. Could they have been "seeing things which weren't there" when they "saw" the risen Christ? Were they the victims of a mass hallucination? The answer to this question must be sought in the realm of the psychology of hallucinations, and we must warn ourselves that our present knowledge of this mysterious subject is very scanty. But there are two fairly well established facts about hallucinations which are relevant to our question. One is the fact that an hallucination is a peculiarly private thing. One person may have or suffer one, under certain special conditions; but five hundred people—all at once—all seeing the same thing that isn't there? This would be a fantastically unusual phenomenon, to say the least. The other fact about hallucinations is that if a person is to see something that isn't there he must have some kind of prior conviction that he is going to see it; and all the evidence suggests that the friends of Jesus did not expect to see Him alive again after His death. They were broken-hearted on the crucifixion day because they were sure they had seen the last of Him. In sum, it is reasonable to conclude that none of the necessary conditions of an hallucination were present.

Other objections have been raised by skeptics. Back in the eighteenth century many rationalists argued, without a shred of evidence, that the disciples stole the body from the tomb. How they could have got past the Roman guard stationed at the tomb was not explained. It has been argued that the body was stolen by others, either Jews or Romans. But if it had been stolen by Jews, they could have spiked the whole Christian story simply by producing the corpse; and if it had been stolen by Romans, the Christians would have had no basis for their claim of a resurrection and the Romans would almost certainly have spiked their story in the same simple way—by producing the corpse in evidence.

The Christians claimed that the tomb was empty. Had it not been empty, if the body had been still there, it would have been a very simple matter for the enemies of the Christian movement to open the tomb and show to the world the dead body.

It may be hard to believe that Jesus rose living from the dead; but when we consider the alternative possibilities it appears at least as hard to believe that He remained dead in the grave. The witnesses for the resurrection tell at least as plausible a story as any that their opponents tell.

Of more convincing weight as evidence to many modern Christians, this writer among them, is the revolutionary consequence of the resurrection. In the analogy of William's conquest of England, mentioned earlier in this chapter, we see a drastic difference between England before 1066 and England after 1066. This may not be absolutely incontestable proof that William conquered England in 1066, but it is enough to throw a very heavy burden of disproof upon anybody who might question it.

The great consequence of Christ's resurrection is the Christian Church as it has been from the beginning.

The crucifixion of Jesus threw His disciples into utter despair and abject terror. A few weeks later, they are a little, but inspired, community of people boldly telling the world that their crucified Leader has risen from the dead and is triumphant Lord of all creation. *Something* happened to effect this change. If it was not the resurrection of Jesus, it is up to the disbelievers to tell us what it was.

Those first Christians were all Jews. As Jews, they

were accustomed to keeping the seventh day of the week, our Saturday, as their weekly Lord's day. But from the very beginning of the Christian movement the Lord's day was the first day of the week, our Sunday. This was because it was the resurrection day. Nothing less than an event of revolutionary impact could have brought about this change.

Along with Sunday as the holy day was kept the original Christian Eucharist—the breaking of bread. If this had been only a ritual commemoration of our Lord's last supper with His disciples before His death, it would have been an occasion of intolerable sadness; but they broke the bread with gladness of heart. Clearly they were convinced that their risen and living Lord was with them in their fellowship-meal with Him and with one another in Him. This made sense only on the premise that He was not dead but living.

This conviction that Christ was with them, not as a hallowed memory but as a living and personal presence, was the very life of the community of believers. This is what made them the Church militant on earth. They could never have poured out their lives in joyful and indomitable devotion had they not been sure that their Lord was risen and living, to make them more than conquerors over all their foes—even death itself. And from that day to this, this experience of communion with the living Christ has been the life and power of the Church.

The New Testament accounts of the resurrection of Christ vary in minor details, but they agree substantially upon the following version of what happened:

When Jesus died on the cross, His soul experienced what every soul experiences upon separation from the body—it descended into Sheol. (Recall the concept of Sheol-Hades described in Chapter 2.) His body was buried in a tomb which belonged to the wealthy Joseph of Arimathea. On the third day after this, according to the Jewish manner of reckoning days—actually about forty hours after His death—the soul and body of Jesus were re-united by the power of God, and He emerged living from His tomb. He showed Himself alive to the faithful women who had come to the tomb to anoint His body, and to Peter and the other apostles. At some later time He showed Himself to the large company of disciples of whom St. Paul speaks. He remained on earth in bodily and visible form for forty days after His resurrection, then removed this bodily presence from the eyes of men to "ascend" into heaven.

The resurrection-body of Christ was the same body in which His friends had known Him before His death, but it had been transformed and glorified. He ate in their presence, to convince them of the reality of His bodily being; yet He did not require food to sustain life (*St. Luke 24:43*; *St. John 21:13* and *Acts 10:41*). In His resurrection-body He was free from our bondage to space; He could appear suddenly in a locked room (*St. John 20:19*) and He could disappear from sight (*St. Luke 24:31*). His resurrection-body was clearly immortal in itself, and not subject to death.[2]

The scars of His crucifixion were visible upon the resurrection-body, a detail which has profound meaning for Christian faith and devotion, as we shall see in the next chapter.

Before passing from our consideration of the Lord's resurrection-body we should note one fact above all, and that is that the New Testament allows no room for any belief that the resurrection appearances of Jesus were what our psychological jargon calls "subjective." An eminent Christian modernist tells us that "the memory of Jesus quickened into a presence" in the minds of His adoring disciples. This means, in less eloquent but more straightforward language, that the disciples remembered their dead Master so vividly that they imagined He was still with them; hence His presence with them was all in their minds and only in their minds. To say this may make belief in the resurrection easy, but it is also to tear up the New Testament. The only Christian belief is that Christ rose from the dead actually and bodily, not in the pious imaginings of His friends but in the reality of His own personal being. We must say, with St. Paul, "If Christ be not risen, then is our preaching vain, and your faith is also vain." (*I Corinthians 15:14*)

5

Hid with Christ in God

THE RESURRECTION of Christ did much more for the first Christians than to give them the joyful assurance that when they died they would be raised to a new and glorious life with their Lord in heaven. It filled them with the assurance that they were already risen with Him, already sharers with Him in His victory over death. They *felt* the resurrection within themselves. Their experience is perfectly expressed by St. Paul in the passage which we hear as the Epistle at the Easter Eucharist: "If ye then be risen with Christ, seek those things which are above, where Christ sitteth on the right hand of God. Set your affection on things above, not on things on the earth. For ye are dead, and your lives are hid with Christ in God. When Christ, who is our life, shall appear, then shall ye also appear with him in glory." (*Colossians 3:1-4*)

The Christian life is a life of identification with Christ in His loving, suffering, dying and rising again. We are made living members of Him in baptism, partakers of His life in the way that an olive branch grafted into an olive tree becomes a partaker of the life of the tree. This life of Christ which flows into His members is Christ's eternal resurrection-life. Hence our resurrection really begins at our baptism. Our life on earth before our death corresponds to Christ's life on earth before His death. He was tempted; so are we. He suffered; so must we. He died; so must we. And because the world resists Christ as much as it ever did, it follows that the more faithful and true we are to the Christ in us "who is our life," the harder must be our struggle against His foes. But our burden is never that of mere stolid endurance in the hope that God will reward us at last in heaven. Our eyes have seen the glory of Christ's resurrection, and we know that the God who raised Him from the dead is ever faithful. But heaven is sharing in the life of Christ, and for the Christian it begins here and now. "Your lives are hid with Christ in God," St. Paul reminds us. If we are now in Christ, we are raised with Him and we are with Him now in heaven.

The life eternal is the life of communion and fellowship with Jesus Christ. It can, and it must, begin in this present life. The death of the body is not done away with by our union with Him, but it is swallowed up in His victory so that when death comes to the faithful Christian it is an episode and a transition from a limited life to a life of infinitely closer companionship with Him. All genuinely Christian thinking about this life and the life to come must follow this line of thought and conception, and it is this line that we are trying to follow in this study.

If our present lives are conformed to Christ in His suffering, our lives in the world to come will be conformed to Him in His glory, and for some clue concerning this we look to Him in His resurrection. His resurrection-body in which He appeared to His friends is a symbol of the life that shall be ours. His words to the grieving Martha at the grave of Lazarus imply this: "I am the resurrection and the life; he that believeth in me, though he were dead, yet shall he live." (*St. John 11:25*) St. Paul has this same understanding of the matter: "As in Adam all die, even so in Christ shall all be made alive." (*I Cor. 15:22*) If we resemble Adam, the natural man, in our dying, we shall resemble Christ in our resurrection-life. We find a most eloquent expression of the same idea in the first Epistle of St. John (*3:2*): "Beloved, now are we the sons of God, and it doth not yet appear what we shall be: but we know that, when he shall appear, we shall be like him, for we shall see him as he is."

When our Lord appeared to His disciples during the great forty days between His resurrection and His ascension He gave us a glimpse of Himself "as he is," with the assurance that "we shall be like him." With this in mind, Christians may meditate upon the risen body of their Lord with the understanding that their own resurrection-life will be in His likeness. Let us then take note of the most significant facts.

We begin with the fact of the empty tomb. A Moslem once taunted a Christian by saying "Our religion is better authenticated than yours is, because we know where the tomb of our Prophet is, and you have no tomb of Jesus." The Christian replied, "You are right. We have no tomb, because we have no corpse." The first Christians proclaimed this very thing to the world as a sign and assurance of God's victory through Jesus Christ. The emptiness of the tomb means that the Man who died is no longer dead.

Does this mean, then, that if our resurrection corresponds to His, our tombs will be literally emptied— that the dust and ashes of our "earthly remains" will be miraculously restored to the physical life and being which we now know as life in the flesh? Not necessarily, although countless Christians have believed this, and still do. But Christ's resurrection had to be, in the nature of the case, a dramatic and convincing sign to us, and it may be that in God's design this was the best way to give it to us: by showing us an empty tomb as proof that Christ is risen. It means, at the very least, that He who rose again is the same person as He who died on the cross and was buried. This is what matters most to us.

The Lord's risen body was unique in some respects, and necessarily so, since He was the first man to be raised from the dead, He had to show Himself to His brethren in such a way that they would understand God's purpose to raise all men likewise. His risen body was the same as His crucified body, yet it had been changed. To say that it had been sublimated or etherealized helps little, since we know of no other body that has undergone the same experience. The two signal facts about it are the facts of its *identity* with the original body and its *change* into a new and glorious form.

Evidently His closest friends did not recognize Him immediately upon seeing Him. In St. Luke's beautiful story of the Lord's walk to Emmaus with two of His disciples it appears that they learned only gradually who their Companion was. (*St. Luke 24:13-31*) It was their faith and love which finally brought joyful recognition. Throughout the New Testament it is asserted that such faith is an indispensable prerequisite to the vision of the risen Lord. Without faith it is impossible to know Him in the glory of His resurrection. We see Him now, we shall see Him face to face in the world to come, only as faith opens our eyes to behold Him.

The next item to consider in this matter of the recognition of the risen Lord is the scars upon His risen body. (*St. Luke 24:40*; *St. John 20:20, 25-28*) St. Thomas is cured of his doubting when he sees the red wounds of his Master's agony, and in this recognition Thomas represents us all. But adoring Christians have always seen in these scars upon the Lord's risen body more than mere visible evidence that this is the same person as the Crucified. As William Temple put it,

"The wounds of Christ are His credentials to the suffering race of men. . . . Only a God in whose perfect Being pain has its place can win and hold our worship; for otherwise the creature would in fortitude surpass the Creator."[3]

As with Him, so with us: the wounds we suffer in the faithful doing of God's will become decorations of honor which we shall wear through all eternity. Whatever pains we must endure in our present life, as true followers of Christ, work for us, as St. Paul declares, "a far more exceeding and eternal weight of glory." (*II Cor. 4:17*) The glorified Christ is more glorious because of His scars. Whatever glory may await us, it will be the sum and consequence of the sufferings of this present time. Hence no labor and no wounds can be in vain, if we are faithful followers of Christ from His humiliation to His exaltation.

It is made clear in the Gospels that the body of the risen Lord was not any kind of ghost, but a truly embodied spirit. To demonstrate this, He ate physical food with His witnesses. *St. Luke 24:39-43*) This again is something that can be explained as a part of the unique situation: He had to convince His witnesses of the *reality* of His resurrection-body, and this was a most effective way of doing it. But like everything else He did, it had also the purpose of teaching us something about what our own resurrection entails. A Negro spiritual sings that in the Kingdom of God "We will break bread together on our knees." We shall have real bodies, enabling us to share the social joys symbolized by eating together.

We may sum up the New Testament testimony concerning the Lord's resurrection-body by saying that Christ was definitely the same person before and after His resurrection, but that after the resurrection His body has been raised and glorified to a condition in which it is no longer subject to the limitations of this earthly life as we know it. It cannot sicken, or decay with the years, or die. What this implies for our resurrection-bodies is well expressed in a verse of one of our hymns:

O how glorious and resplendent,
   Fragile body, shalt thou be,
When endued with heav'nly beauty,
   Full of health, and strong, and free,
Full of vigor, full of pleasure
   That shall last eternally![4]

All our thinking about our life after death, which will be a new and higher stage of our eternal life, must be speculative, and we can express our ideas of it only in imaginative terms. Some modern Christians go so far as to say that it is a mistake to do this at all. In my judgment, they push their objection too far when they condemn much of our hymnody for its imaginative picturing of heaven, saying that it encourages an unchristian other-worldliness which distracts us from the duties of this present life. This charge seems inhuman. As human beings who believe that our Father in heaven has in store for His faithful children a "glorious and resplendent" life in His nearer presence, it is both natural and right that we should try to imagine what it will be like. And our best "heavenly Jerusalem" hymns set before us a vision of heaven which is not unworthy of our Christian hopes:

There lust and lucre cannot dwell;
   There envy bears no sway;
There is no hunger, heat, nor cold,
   But pleasure every way.

*   *   *

Truly Jerusalem name we that shore,
Vision of peace that brings joy evermore;
Wish and fulfilment can sever'd be ne'er,
Nor the thing prayed for come short of the prayer.

*   *   *

O then what raptur'd greetings
On Canaan's happy shore!
What knitting sever'd friendships up,
Where partings are no more!
Then eyes with joy shall sparkle,
That brimmed with tears of late;
Orphans no longer fatherless,
Nor widows desolate.[5]

Such joys as are thus described are entirely implicit in our Lord's promise: "In my Father's house are many mansions: if it were not so, I would have told you. I go to prepare a place for you." (*St. John 14:2*)

Nevertheless, if our thinking about the eternal life is entirely futuristic it is not Christian thinking. In His great high-priestly prayer, recorded by St. John, Jesus identifies the life eternal with the true knowledge of God: "And this is life eternal, that they might know thee the only true God, and Jesus Christ, whom thou hast sent." (*St. John 17:3*) This knowledge of God, which is our eternal life, is our present Christian knowledge of Him, however dim and undeveloped it may be; and to have this knowledge now is to have eternal life now. "Knowledge" in this biblical sense is not mere intellectual apprehension of truth, like one's knowledge of the multiplication table; rather it is the knowledge of a person which comes from living with that person and coming to know him as he is. To know God through Jesus Christ is to live with God as Christ reveals Him to us and thus to enter into our Lord's filial relationship to the Father. To do this is to realize, ever more and more strongly as we walk with Him, that He is indeed our Father and that in His house is our eternal home.

There is, to be sure, a great difference between the eternal life as the Christian knows it in the flesh and the eternal life as the saints in heaven know it. It is the difference between the seed and the full-grown plant. The eternal life in heaven is the glorious fruition and completion of what Jesus Christ begins in us here and now. But it is the same life, here and yonder, in two different stages. And it is strengthened or weakened in us by our own faithfulness or faithlessness as followers of Christ. The following analogy is suggested by an English theologian:

"Every act of self-surrender increases the life that is in us, and conversely every selfish act diminishes our true vitality. The Japanese, we are told, have a punishment which is entitled, 'Death by a thousand cuts': none of the cuts is in itself fatal, but the result is sure. It is hardly fanciful to suggest that a similar result is to be feared from those small, and in themselves trifling, acts of self-assertion and self-pleasing which most of us daily commit. Those who indulge in them are described in the Second Epistle to the Corinthians (4:3) . . . as 'those that are perishing,' whose thoughts and minds 'the God of this world hath blinded.' They supply the antithesis to 'them that are being saved,' who are advancing day by day in that knowledge of God which can only come by self-surrender." [6]

In an earlier chapter, we considered those intimations of immortality which seem to be innate in all mankind—the feeling, the intuition, that there is "something beyond." There is a beautiful expression

58 ৡৼ

of this in Charles Dickens' *Dombey and Son*. Little Paul Dombey, who is soon to die, is visiting the seashore with his devoted sister Florence, and the following conversation takes place:

"Quaking suddenly, he listened, started up, and sat listening. Florence asked him what he thought he heard.

'I want to know what it says,' he answered, looking steadily in her face. 'The sea, Floy, what is it that it keeps on saying?'

She told him that it was only the noise of the rolling waves.

'Yes, yes,' he said. 'But I know that they are always saying something. Always the same thing. What place is over there?' He rose up, looking eagerly at the horizon.

She told him that there was another country opposite, but he said he didn't mean that: he meant farther away—farther away!

Very often afterwards, in the midst of their talk, he would break off, to try to understand what it was that the waves were always saying; and would rise up in his couch to look towards that invisible region, far away."

Little Paul's intuition of the invisible region far away is confirmed, corroborated, substantiated by what we learn from God when we faithfully serve Jesus Christ and thus gain that knowledge which is the beginning of our eternal life. It is well expressed by the poet Percy Ainsworth in these verses:

It is not something yet to be revealed—
The everlasting life—'tis here and now;
Passing unseen because our eyes are sealed
With blindness for the pride upon our brow.

It dwells not in innumerable years;
It is the breath of God in timeless things—
The strong, divine persistence that inheres
In love's red pulses and in faith's white wings.

It is the power whereby low lives aspire
Unto the doing of a selfless deed,
Unto the slaying of a soft desire,
In the service of a high, unworldly creed.

It is the treasure that is ours to hold
Secure, while all things else are turned to dust;
That priceless and imperishable gold
Beyond the scathe of robber and of rust.

And if we feel it not amid our strife,
In all our toiling and in all our pain—
The rhythmic pulsing of eternal life—
Then do we work and suffer here in vain.

If our lives are truly hid with Christ in God at the present moment, if we are giving our best and our all to His faithful service, we know that we have passed from death to an imperishable life; and if we continue in this way unto our life's end, this knowledge will daily increase.

6

Death and Judgment

"IT IS appointed unto men once to die, but after this the judgment." (*Hebrews 9:27*)

Christianity has no easy and pleasant doctrine of death. It makes no pretense that dying is not real and painful to him who dies and to us who witness his dying. Pascal, a devout Christian, puts it plainly: "The last act is tragic, however happy all the rest of the play is; at the last a little earth is thrown upon our head, and that is the end forever." So far as this present life and world is concerned, it is certainly so. St. Paul calls death "the last enemy" and he predicts that it shall be destroyed at last; but in the meantime it is still with us as an hostile power, and we are in that meantime.

It may well be true that if we could be entirely natural about our dying it would not trouble us as it does; but the simple truth is that we cannot be entirely natural about this, or about anything else, because something has gone wrong with our nature. We are, as somebody has called us, a spoiled species; and Christ's eternal business with us is to restore us to the nature God gave us. We are not natural with God, with one another, with ourselves, and so we cannot be natural with death. If we are believing and living Christians, we are in process of being unspoiled and set right, but we are still sick in spirit and therefore warped in understanding.

Death and the judgment to come are closely linked together in Christian thought. This is not simply because our lives are not finally and decisively judged until after our death, but also because the fact that we must die is itself a part of God's judgment upon us. In making us realize that we do not have forever in which to do His will in this world, God teaches us the eternal importance of whatever we say, think, or do today. The present moment is all that we certainly have. When Felix, the Roman governor, heard the prisoner Paul's impassioned reasoning of "righteousness, temperance, and judgment to come," he trembled and asked Paul to go his way "for this time; when I have a convenient season, I will call for thee." (*Acts 24:25*) Felix wanted to postpone his coming to terms with God until some convenient tomorrow. This is very human, but very unrealistic thinking in a mortal man who may not be given a tomorrow. The realization that we must die, and that this very day our souls may be required of us, stimulates us to such living in the present moment as will enable us to come before the divine Taskmaster at the end of our day with something to show for our stewardship. St. Augustine testified: "Nothing has contributed more to wean me away from an idle preoccupation with trivial things than the thought of death and the last account." Even our Lord Himself lived by this rule: "I must work the works of him that sent me, while it is day: the night cometh, when no man can work." (*St. John 9:4*)

It is by the deeds done in our flesh that we are judged, and death marks the end of our flesh. This conviction is elemental to a Christian understanding of our life in time and in eternity: "once to die, and after this the judgment." To believe this is not to preclude the possibility of our growth and development after death, but it is to affirm that the eternal direction and destiny of our lives is cast in the here-and-now, for better or for worse. We depart from this life with our faces turned toward Christ or away from Him; and it is precisely our life-reaction to Him which is the judgment.

Christ's judgment of us is actually a lifelong process culminating at the last in a final summing up, and we believe that in our face-to-face confrontation with Him as we enter eternity we shall see ourselves as we are for the first time. As Newman expressed it in *Dream of Gerontius*, "The *shame of self* at thought of seeing Him, shall be thy keenest, sharpest Purgatory." And Whittier: "Thou judgest us: thy purity doth all our lusts condemn."

Christian theologians have usually distinguished between the particular judgment, which immediately follows death, and the general judgment at the end of the world. This distinction we shall now consider; but before doing so we should remind ourselves of something very important to all clear thinking about the life beyond death. It is this: that in eternity there can be no sequence of events in an order of past, present, and future. But, because in our present life we cannot think in any other terms, we must think of the eternal realities in a temporal and spatial way. This means that we must think of the particular judgment upon each individual life as coming *before* the general judgment, because only thus can we make it meaningful to ourselves. Yet "before" and "after" are terms of time rather than of eternity. For the same reason, we are forced to think of heaven as some kind of *place*—geographically conceived, as a city or a country occupying space. Such pictorial thinking about the world to come is necessary, and by no means false in itself; but we should always keep in mind that it is just this—imaginative, impressionistic, and, in the true sense, mythological. (The purpose of a true myth is to express a truth which cannot be expressed in a direct and definitive way.)

The particular judgment is the experience in which a person's life is brought into the immediate presence of Christ at his death and is there revealed to the individual as it truly is. We do not know our own selves as we really are; not now. But we shall, when we stand before Christ. As one of the theologians has put it: Christ's judgment does not change the judged, it simply shows them, reveals them. The person knows then what his eternal destiny is. He has become, for all eternity, what he chose to become in his life on earth.

What happens "then?" (We put "then" in quotation marks to remind ourselves that we are using temporal language for the sake of our present understanding, rather than to suggest that there can be a "then," "now," or "later" in eternity.) Many people are fond of the idea that one may be given a "second chance" in the life to come. They point out that an individual in his earthly life may have had no knowledge of Christ and little or no opportunity to serve God, and they argue that a just and merciful God would not deprive anybody of a fair chance to know, love, and serve Him. This reasoning comes out of a commendable desire to be just to God as well as to man, but it must be rejected as fallacious. The New Testament teaching is that a person is judged by his use of whatever light and opportunity is given to him. If little is given to one, little shall be required of him by the just Judge. We have every right to believe that if a person's life, with all its failures and all its ignorance and lack of opportunity, has been turned toward the light of Christ, that person will be given an opportunity to grow and develop, to press on toward the goal which is set before him in the perfect life of Christ. But this is not a "second chance"; rather it is a chance to become what one chose to become, in his inmost being. It is easy to think of hard cases to test this principle. What of the poor soul who is born a hopeless idiot? How can he exercise any decisive choice for or against God—even subconsciously? We do not know, of course. But the Lord knows, and we are sure that He who knows the secrets of all hearts is both perfectly just and infinitely kind. The Christian principle stands: that our eternal destiny is fixed by our present reaction to Christ, for Him or against Him.

What happens to either the lost or to the saved at the particular judgment is not revealed to us. We must remember that this is not the end. Whatever it is, the condition of departed souls between the particular judgment and the general judgment must have some eternal correspondence to what we who live in time call waiting, anticipation, and preparation. We may call this condition the intermediate state.

Since our friends and loved ones who have died are now presumably in this condition of awaiting the general resurrection and the last judgment, we are naturally interested in this mystery. We believe that they whose final destiny is heaven are being prepared for that glorious end, and the Episcopal Church maintains the Catholic belief that our departed friends can be helped by our prayers just as they could be helped while in the flesh. Hence we pray at the Eucharist that God will grant them "continual growth" in His love and service. (Prayer Book, page 75. Other prayers for the departed are to be found in the Burial Office, and the beautiful prayer "For an Anniversary of One Departed" on page 598.) We recall our Lord's promise to the dying thief: "Today thou shalt be with me in paradise." (*St. Luke 23:43*) Paradise is the condition of waiting and preparation for heaven. What this experience of preparation may consist of is beyond our present imagining, and we must be content to leave it to God.

At the end comes the resurrection of "the quick and the dead" and the last judgment upon them. It will come in God's good time, and at a time that we cannot anticipate. All creation waits for it.

Christ gives us very full teaching concerning the end of the world and the last judgment, but His teaching is necessarily given to us in pictorial metaphor. The essential points of His doctrine may be summarized thus:

Christ Himself will be the judge. (*St. Matthew 16:27* and *25:32*; *Acts 17:31*) He is perfectly fitted to this office by being both God and man. (*St. John 5:27*) His deity assures us that He knows all things and is perfectly just, so that He cannot judge us ignorantly or unjustly. His being man assures us that He knows from His human experience all of our mortal weaknesses and limitations.

All men and nations will be judged. (*St. Matthew 25:32*; *I Cor. 6:3*; *Rev. 20:10*; *Jude 6*; *II Peter 2:4*) All men—and all human affairs and relationships—will be arraigned before Christ.

The one and only principle of judgment will be that of acceptability to Christ. Is the person, or the nation, or the labor union, or the peace treaty, or the poem, or the marriage, for Him or against Him? The judge is Himself the criterion; He is the judgment.

This judgment will be final. Whoever and whatever is rejected "shall go away into everlasting punishment: but the righteous into life eternal." (*St. Matthew 25:46*)

The logical order of the last things is the second coming of Christ to earth, the resurrection of the dead, and the general judgment. We must think of these as events in sequence, but from an eternal point of view they are a single action.

Christ's numerous recorded statements concerning His coming at the end of this world have one general admonitory import: that we are to live in constant readiness for it. The Christian rule is to live, God helping us, as though this day may well be the last day for us and for all creation.

He teaches clearly that the bodies of the dead will rise again. (*St. Mark 12:25, St. Luke 20:37*) He does not teach, however, that this resurrection will involve a physical restoration and re-animation of the flesh-and-blood organism which we now regard as the body. St. Paul explicitly distinguishes between our present body, which he calls the natural body, and the spiritual body which is raised. (*I Cor. 15:42-44*) Perhaps the best way of thinking about this is to say that the present body we now have is our *self* as God has fitted and adapted the self to its life in this physical and temporal stage of our existence, while the spiritual body we shall receive will be the same self, the same person, but now fitted and adapted to the conditions of life in the world to come. The essential point is that the identity of the self is preserved through the great change: John Smith remains John Smith, and recognizably, unalterably so, forever.

7

Hell

T HERE IS a widespread and mischievous notion in our world that Christianity is like a department store in which one can browse pleasantly, taking what he wants and leaving what he doesn't want. This idea gets pseudo-scientific support from that pseudo-psychology which holds that a thing is good if it makes you feel good and bad if it makes you feel bad. Where this notion prevails, the Christian doctrine of hell is naturally one of those items which the shopper is content to leave on the shelf: he just isn't "buying" it.

This whole approach is totally unreasonable as well as totally unchristian. Christianity is that truth of God which Jesus reveals and teaches—*all of it*. He teaches that there is hell, that hell is eternal punishment, and that it is the sure consequence of rejecting Him.

The Gospels record many sayings of Jesus on the subject of hell, but before we come to these we should remind ourselves what His Gospel is and what it implies concerning man's reaction to it. "Now after that John was put in prison, Jesus came into Galilee, preaching the gospel of the kingdom of God, and saying, The time is fulfilled, and the kingdom of God is at hand: repent ye, and believe the gospel." (*St. Mark 1:14-15*) The glorious good news of the Gospel is that the kingdom of heaven, the joy and life of becoming God's beloved Children, stands open to all believers. They have only to repent—to change their ways to God's Way, to accept the kingdom and to enter in.

But what if they do not? There can be no compulsion in this. What God wants is our *wills*. In Tennyson's words, "Our wills are ours, to make them thine." These we can give to God only if we *will* to give them. God can invite us to His kingdom; He will not compel us to come. God can show us the glory of life in His Kingdom. He can remove all barriers to our entrance. He can die on a cross to win us to it. All these things He has done, and more, through Jesus Christ our Lord. But having done all that He can do from His side, He will leave the decision to us.

This is something that any child can understand. The child knows that his parents can teach him how to be good and they can give him every incentive to be good; but the actual being good is up to him alone. If we believe that we are in the same case under God, we must believe in hell.

Thus we come to our essential definition. *Hell is alienation from God through our rejection of His rule in our lives.* George Macdonald rightly says that the essential principle of hell is "I am my own!" Where God's will is done, there is heaven; where God's will is not done, there is hell. Jesus on the Cross is in heaven. The crucifiers in their "triumph" are in hell.

The example just cited points up a very important

fact. It is that one's feelings at the moment are no reliable clue to whether one is in heaven or in hell. Happiness, as the word is normally understood, is not the criterion. It can be argued, and Christians do argue with full conviction, that the heavenly way of loving submission to the Father's will in all things is the way of life and peace. The writer of the Epistle to the Hebrews reminds us that it was for the joy that was set before Him that Jesus endured the Cross. (*Hebrews 12:2*) Conversely it can be said that the way of hell, the way of living by the principle "I am my own," is the way to the death of that joy for which we are made—the joy of the children of God revelling in the treasures of their Father's house. But this is not to deny that a person might have a taste for hell rather than for heaven. A man reared on swine husks rather than on the fare of princes may acquire a permanent preference for husks. He may never know what he is missing.

The first principle is, then, that heaven and hell are conditions which have their beginning in our present life, and are the consequences of our voluntary response to God's call to us to give Him our wills. Heaven begins with the acceptance of God's will as the rule of our living, hell begins with the acceptance of self-will as our rule of action. The choice need not be fully deliberate. To be sure, the chooser presumably knows the difference between good and bad as Christ spells it out for us. Our Lord shows us clearly what is good and well-pleasing in God's sight. None the less it is true that we can easily ignore what we know, when it is inconvenient or costly in its demands upon us, and we can reject it—not with the purpose of going to hell but simply for the purpose of doing something easier and more attractive. In C. S. Lewis' *Screwtape Letters*, Screwtape, a bureaucrat of hell's "Lowerarchy," is counselling a young nephew whose job on earth is to lure a Christian to the realm of "Our Father Below." Among his shrewd counsels is this:

"It does not matter how small the sins are, provided that their cumulative effect is to edge the man away from the Light and out into the Nothing. Murder is no better than cards if cards can do the trick. Indeed the safest road to Hell is the gradual one—the gentle slope, soft underfoot, without sudden turnings, without milestones, without signposts." [7]

The Fourth Gospel makes the essential principle specific in these words: "And this is the condemnation, that light is come into the world, and men loved darkness rather than light, because their deeds were evil. For every one that doeth evil hateth the light, neither cometh to the light, lest his deeds should be reproved." (*St. John 3:19-20*) Christ is the light, and He is here in our world. If men do not want their evil to be burned away by that light they will stay away from Him. But to stay away from the light is to abide in darkness; we cannot have it both ways. This darkness is hell. Christ describes Himself as the light of the world (*St. John 9:5*), and as the resurrection and the life. (*St. John 11:25*) If His claim is true, we have light and life only as we choose to give our lives over to Him, body and soul. The only alternative is darkness and living death—hell.

All that we have said thus far applies to our present life, certainly; but what of the life to come? Can it be that our rejection of Christ, with the spiritual consequences thereof, may become final and eternal and last beyond death?

The teaching of Jesus gives an unambiguous and affirmative answer. St. Luke preserves for us Christ's parable of the rich man and Lazarus who died and went to their appointed places. (*St. Luke 16:19-31*) As we have earlier noted (page 33 *supra*), this story is not intended to give us a photographic description of the world to come, but rather to awaken our conscience to our present duty: nevertheless it is inconceivable that Jesus would have told such a parable if the story which frames the meaning is totally false to the eternal realities. In the story the rich man goes to hell, because of his neglect of God's commandments while in his earthly life; and he is punished with what he calls "this flame." Elsewhere in the Gospels Jesus speaks of hell's "unquenchable fire" (*St. Mark 9:43* RSV), or "eternal fire" (*St. Matthew 18:8* RSV), or the casting of the wicked into the "furnace of fire." (*St. Matthew 13:42* RSV)

To be sure, this is symbolic language—if that is any comfort to us. But it has a real and awful meaning to anybody who takes it seriously, as the Christian must. This symbolism must be understood, not explained away. In the Bible, fire symbolizes the destruction of that which God rejects. This metaphor probably stems out of the destruction by fire of the doomed cities of Sodom and Gomorrah. (*Genesis 9:24*) Unquestionably this is what Jesus has in mind when He speaks of

76 ঽঌ

the fire of hell. But fire in this biblical symbol has another implication, which is clearly suggested in the story of Lazarus. The rich man is tormented by remorse. In hell he sees what he ought to have been, and he begs "Father Abraham" to send Lazarus from heaven to earth to warn his five brothers "lest they also come into this place of torment." Dean Harry N. Hancock offers a helpful elucidation of this aspect of the punishing fire:

"Perhaps we can laugh at that 'mixture of buffoonery and savagery' which constituted the medieval idea of hell, with its fire and flames and shrieks of agony. Perhaps we can afford to make jokes and tell funny stories about it, because we feel that it has no reality. But what of the fires of hatred, greed and envy, malice and jealousy that burn so insatiably in the human heart? We all know how real they are, and most of us have felt at least a touch of the pain they cause; and if, in the words of Jesus, 'Their worm dieth not [the worm of gnawing desire increasingly incapable of satisfaction] and their fire is not quenched'—the fire of burning lust or hate or jealousy—then that is Hell even worse and far more real than Dante's wildest dreams. Nor do we have to wait for death before we feel a foretaste of it. We can hardly afford to laugh at that, for Hell is as real as man's ugliest passions, and Heaven as his purest love." [8]

It is implicit in the whole Christian understanding of man and his destiny that a person is eternally what he chooses to become in time: and his reaction to

Christ, for Him or against Him, is the determining factor; it is the judgment; it is the basis of the eternal verdict. *What we are now becoming we shall be forever.* The old saying that "heaven begun is half won" holds equally true of hell. The great English mystic, William Law, put the Christian view of the matter thus:

"Men are not in Hell because God is angry with them: they are in wrath and darkness because they have done to the light which infinitely flows forth from God, as that man does to the light of the sun who puts out his own eyes."

We considered earlier (pages 64-65) the question of a possible "second chance" in eternity for people who have failed to accept the heavenly life from Christ in time. Another word needs to be said concerning that. The highest Christian saint on earth realizes with sorrow that much still needs to be done with him before he can be ready for the full joy and the beatific vision of God in heaven. We have every right to believe that God will give us opportunity to finish becoming in eternity what we have chosen to become on earth. But that choice must be made—earnestly and decisively made —and made here and now. Our life as a whole is a vote for Christ, or against Him: which is to say, for heaven or for hell. The Christian belief in an intermediate state, or Paradise, or purgatory, is not a doctrine of a second chance but rather of a further chance to become what we have chosen to become as aspiring children of God.

There are certain questions which invariably present themselves when Christians think seriously about eternal salvation and eternal rejection. The most obvious one is: Who is saved and who is lost? Who goes to heaven and who goes to hell? The only answer must be: God only knows. No Christian has any right to take his ultimate salvation simply for granted. St. Paul, as a Christian, had better reason than most to believe that his heroic labors for the cause of Christ might "earn" heaven for him; but he knew the ways of God too well to suppose that he or anybody could work his way to heaven by his own good works. He knew that he had accepted the good-news of God in Christ which by itself saves a man for this life and the life to come; but what he could not be sure of was his own self, that he would persevere in this way of salvation to the end; and so he declares: "But I keep under my body, and bring it into subjection: lest that by any means, when I have preached to others, I myself should be a castaway." (*I Cor. 9:27*) He regarded his own possible final damnation as a very live option; and elsewhere (*Romans 11:22*) he speaks of both "the goodness and severity of God." The severity of God means that He is not mocked, that whatever a man sows that shall he reap. If a man sows the seeds of his own destruction, he shall reap his own destruction. When we say that only God knows who makes this choice we mean simply and literally that. Only God knows the secrets of every heart. Our Lord's precept "Judge not, that ye be not judged" is simple realism. We are incapable of judging anybody, in the sense of declaring whether heaven or hell is his present condition or future destination, because we cannot see his inner life and the direction of his soul. So long as a person is responding to the grace of God, he is moving heavenward; so long as he is spurning the grace of God and walking in his own way, he is moving hellward. That is all we know, and all we need to know.

There is one other question which thoughtful Christians must ponder. Is hell an everlasting punishment, or does it come to an end at last in either the total extinction of the soul or its release from its torment? Concerning this, we must remind ourselves of the truth we have already considered (page 64f.), that we must not suppose that in eternity there are periods of time as we now experience them. Hence to say that a person might spend some time in hell before being totally destroyed, or before being moved up to a better state, is meaningless.

Nevertheless, there may be something corresponding to such changes in eternity. Bishop Charles Gore and some other great and orthodox theologians have maintained the view that some souls may experience total destruction in hell. Bishop Gore reasons thus:

"Final ruin may involve, I cannot but think, such a dissolution of personality as carries with it the cessation of personal consciousness. In this way the final ruin of irretrievably lost spirits, awful as it is to contemplate, may be found consistent with St. Paul's anticipation of a universe in which God is to be all in all —which does not seem to be really compatible with the existence of a region of everlastingly tormented rebellious spirits." [9]

This is a plausible theory, which squares with both the goodness of God and the power of God to accomplish His own loving purposes. But it is only a theory. Other Christian thinkers have held that the eternal punishment of the wicked is "everlasting" in the sense that it will never come to an end. This also is a theory.

What is fact is that our Lord warns us to fear not him who has power to destroy our bodies only, but rather to fear him who can cast both body and soul into hell. That can happen to us, if we let it happen: and we can.

8

Heaven

A ROMAN CATHOLIC theologian describes heaven in terms which must be acceptable to any fully believing Christian:

"The Christian looks forward to heaven as his *home*, not simply as a place of happiness which he may reach if he is fortunate. Incorporated in Christ who reigns in glory, a true son of God, made already a sharer in the life of God, he may look forward to eternal happiness as the completion of God's loving plan for him; and so in a calm spirit of hope and love he awaits the day of the Lord, not as a day of wrath and vengeance but as a day of home-coming." [10]

The emphasis in this fine statement is sound and right. It is placed on the fact that in our present life in the flesh, as Christians, we come to know God through Christ in such a way that we can be truly "at home" with Him. No longer is He a stranger to us; He is our Father. We are at home with God in Christ— "hid with God in Christ." We find in Him, as the familiar hymn expresses it, "our shelter from the stormy blast—and our eternal home." Our present knowledge of God is only rudimentary at best, but it is enough, if it is Christian knowledge, to make us increasingly sure as we walk through time toward eternity that we do indeed belong with Him.

Heaven is best thought of as the state of being perfectly and completely at home with God. The fullness of heaven is not available to us in our present life, for the simple reason that we are not ready for it. God is like any good human parent, in giving to His children enlarged freedoms and His intimate confidence only as they grow up into readiness for them. To give a ten-year-old boy the freedom of the family automobile would be a cruel kindness. When he has reached eighteen, if he seems ready for it, the gift of this freedom is in order. If we, being evil, know how to give good gifts to our children in this good way, how much more does God! Heaven, I repeat, is best thought of as the state of being perfectly at home with God; and this implies that in heaven His children have grown up to such spiritual adulthood that they can be trusted with the glorious liberty of God Himself. The joy of heaven must consist, fundamentally, of the realization that God no longer treats us as babes but can take us into His confidence as His grown-up sons and daughters.

Since we are still in God's kindergarten, it is natural enough that we should hold childish ideas of heaven at our present stage, but we need to realize that they are that and that we need to try to grow out of them. Thomas Moore describes the Moslem idea of heaven in this unflattering couplet:

> A Persian's heaven is easily made:
> 'Tis but black eyes and lemonade.

Christians can conceive of heaven in terms no less childish—and selfish—as a place where all of one's present desires are fulfilled without effort and without limit.

Much of our thinking about heaven as our eternal reward is childish. A small child may try to be good throughout this whole week because he is working for a trip to the circus as his reward. The promise of the circus is a bribe. It is easy for us to think of heaven in the same fashion, as a reward that we can earn. This makes the promise of heaven, "if we are good," a bribe. The New Testament holds forth no such doctrine. The true and only reward of the good person, in the Christian sense, is that of becoming a really, completely good person, which he knows to his sorrow that he is not now. "Blessed are they that hunger and thirst after righteousness," says our Lord, "for they shall be filled" —with the righteousness they long for above all other treasures. "Blessed are the pure in heart, for they shall see God." This beatitude is the perfect formulation of our Lord's teaching about heaven. To see God is not simply to behold Him face to face, but to be so fully conformed to Him in our own character and being that we are entirely at home with Him.

The childishness that we need to outgrow in our thinking about heaven consists of merely taking the things that we most like or covet in our earthly existence and "eternalizing" them—supposing that whatever we now want we are going to get, in infinite measure, if we reach heaven. Do we want peace, ease, security, luxury, success, victory over our rivals and enemies —the "black eyes and lemonade" of the Moslem's dream? The childish reasoning is that we shall get them in heaven, and that those nasty people whom we don't like will not get them. All such thinking is wrong, and worse than wrong, for it confirms in us that selfish spiritual infantilism which propels us toward hell, not heaven.

How then should we think, as Christians, about heaven? The fundamental realities which should control our thinking are set before us in the closing articles of the Apostles Creed: "the Communion of Saints; the Forgiveness of sins; the Resurrection of the body; and the Life everlasting." If we have a sound understanding of these realities, and their inter-relationships, our thinking about heaven will move in the right direction. So we shall devote the remaining pages of this book to a brief consideration of each.

"To him that is joined to all the living there is hope." So wrote the pessimistic sage known as the Preacher, in *Ecclesiastes*. By "the living" he meant only those who live now in the flesh. A Christian can take his words and mean something very different. By "the living" Christians mean all who are alive unto God, in this life and the life to come; and we have high hope and sure confidence that we are joined to them by a bond of love and mutual concern which not even death can break. This ever living, indestructible community of all souls who belong to Christ, in this life and in the life to come, is the Communion of Saints. We have been baptized and initiated into this community. What it means, for our living and dying and for our departed friends in Christ, is ingeniously expressed by John Donne (1571-1631) in one of his sermons:

"This is the faith that sustains me, when I lose by the death of others, or when I suffer by living in misery myselfe. That the dead and we, are now all in one Church, and at the resurrection, shall be all in one Quire."

Donne's metaphor of a church is very apt. We are at present in the nave of the church, some distance from the heavenly sanctuary wherein God dwells, surrounded by those who have entered His nearer presence; but the time comes when we shall all be gathered together around Him in the choir. Even now, however, we in the earthly nave and they in the heavenly sanctuary make up one congregation, one body of worshipers, one communion and fellowship in the mystical body of Christ.

Do our friends in paradise help us? We may be sure that they do, in ways beyond our knowing. Can we help them? We do not doubt it; we can pray for them and commend them to God's continuing care and love, just as we do for our friends still in the flesh. For it is above all a community of mutual love and care and help. We believe that the faithful in paradise experience the joy of the Communion of Saints much more fully than we do, because they have advanced to the higher stage of it. "We feebly struggle, they in glory shine." William Temple rightly reminds us:

"There is not now that interpenetration of personality between those on earth and those who have died which we do to some extent experience in our relations with those whom we love most on earth. It can only be when freed from the limitations of our earthly existence that we enter into the very fulness of the joy of the Lord, which is the joy of perfected love." [11]

In other words, love longs for perfect union with the beloved, and such perfect union is not possible to us in this present life. But the Communion of Saints, as we so imperfectly realize it on earth, is a pledge, a foretaste, and an assurance of the perfect union in love, with our Lord and with those who are in Him, which we shall attain to at last and enjoy forever.

In our thinking about the Last Things, we commonly forget to consider the forgiveness of sins as a relevant matter; but the Creed is right in putting this article of our faith just where it does, along with the Communion of Saints and the resurrection of the body. For we cannot hope to remain and to advance in the Communion of Saints, and we cannot hope to share in the resurrection to the life everlasting, except as we are forgiven. We are not worthy of God's gift of eternal life; we cannot hope to earn it by our own moral achievement. We are poor sinners who must be forgiven.

The Gospel as the Apostles received it from our Lord and proclaimed it to the world was a twofold promise: God's forgiveness and God's gift of eternal life through Jesus Christ our Lord. When God forgives us, He receives us as His own beloved children; and His receiving us in pardoning love is our assurance of life everlasting in the Father's house.

This good news of God's forgiveness may seem to us such "old news" that we casually take it for granted. Indeed, the Christian who has been taught the wonderful truth about the God whose property is always to have mercy is peculiarly tempted to be presumptuous about it, to the grave peril of his soul. Heaven is at-homeness with God, in our Father's house; but we cannot be at home with Him except as we receive His forgiveness, and we cannot love Him as we ought except as we see what it costs God to forgive us: and this we see on the Cross. God must resort to this awful sacrifice to reconcile us to Himself. If we can take *this* for granted, receive *this* casually, we are in no mood for heaven. Our forgiveness is not achieved easily; it must not be received lightly. Our road to heaven begins at the foot of the Cross.

God's forgiveness means His receiving us, as the father in our Lord's parable (*St. Luke 15*) receives his errant and penitent son. If we keep this picture in mind and let it govern our thinking about God's receiving us into His house, we shall not go wrong.

In the fifth chapter, we considered the nature of our Lord's resurrection body with its clear implications for our own resurrection experience. Continuing our reflection upon this mystery in the sixth chapter, we summed up the meaning of the Christian's resurrection by saying that "the identity of the self is preserved through the great change: John Smith remains John Smith, and recognizably, unalterably so, forever." John Smith himself is raised from this present life of changes, chances, and sure death at the last, to a life of glorious stability in a fixed abode—an everlasting life.

Heaven is perfect at-homeness with God, and it must be perfect at-homeness with the other children in the

Father's house. We all hope to meet our friends and loved ones in heaven and to enjoy a fuller and richer fellowship with them than is possible on earth. It is a reasonable hope and expectation. I hope that an amusing story at this point will offend no reader's sense of propriety. (It shouldn't, if the reader is a Christian.) The story concerns a devout old professor at a Southern seminary whose Southern patriotism was a part of his religion. One day, while lecturing to his students on the Last Things, he said, "I look forward to death and that time when I can meet the great patriarchs—Abraham, Isaac, and Jacob." Then he drew a long breath and added with emphasis: "Yes, and Stonewall Jackson and Robert E. Lee!" His expectation was entirely Christian.

We should never lose sight of the fact, however, that the great promise of God is that we shall be with *Him*, in the company of all the hosts of heaven. "I go to prepare a place for you," Jesus says to His faithful. "And if I go and prepare a place for you, I will come again, and receive you unto myself; that where I am, there ye may be also." (*St. John 14:2-3*)

Assuming that by the mercy of God we shall reach heaven at last, we ask questions about the nature of the heavenly life even when we know that our answers must be speculative surmises at best. God gives us no detailed information about it, since we could not possibly receive and comprehend it now. The truth is as St. Paul reminds us: "Eye hath not seen, nor ear heard, neither have entered into the heart of man, the things which God hath prepared for them that love him." (*I Corinthians 2:9*)

Yet it would be gravely wrong to say that we know nothing about heaven. God has in fact revealed to us as much as He judges fit for us to know about it now, and this is in fact very substantial knowledge.

In heaven, the redeemed souls reach the final fruition of their own growth in Christ-likeness. As Professor A. E. Taylor once put it: "In the Christian heaven there is no progress, but only fruition; you are at home, and your journeys are over and done with." [12] There are no more "worlds to conquer" within your own being: you have arrived at where God wants you to be in personal character. This may seem to us at our present stage a vision of eternally arrested growth; but, as Dr. Taylor says in considering it:

"To use the language of devout imagination, the winning of heaven would not leave the pilgrim arrived at the end of his journey with nothing further to do. In heaven itself, though there would be no longer progress *towards* fruition, there might well be progress *in* fruition. Life 'there' would be, as life 'here' is not, living by vision, as contrasted with living by faith and hope; but might not the vision itself be capable of ever-increasing enrichment?" [13]

In an exquisite line, Matthew Arnold describes the pervading sound and climate of heaven as "the rustle of the eternal rain of love." The life of heaven is the life of perfected love, received and given in spontaneous and joyful and inexhaustible exchange, between God and His redeemed creatures and among them all. There can be no effort in this love; in our present life we must work hard at loving God and each other be-cause we are not yet perfect in love. The supreme joy of heaven must consist in the ability to love perfectly, without effort and without let or hindrance. There is an old legend, which can always stand re-telling, about a man who was granted a visit to both hell and heaven. In hell he was shown a host of people seated at a huge banquet table laden with wonderful food. Each had a long fork, three feet in length, fastened to his right hand, while his left hand was shackled. The diners were not dining but starving, for none could feed himself with the cumbersome fork. Then he was taken to heaven and was shown a very similar sight, but he noted one great difference: the diners were revelling in the food and the companionship. Then he saw that each diner was feeding the person across the table from him with the long fork. The mechanics of the heavenly life are probably quite different from that; but the es-sence and soul of that life must be as the legend sug-gests. St. John truly expresses the mind of his Master when he testifies: "We know that we have passed from death unto life, because we love the brethren. He that loveth not his brother abideth in death." (*I John 3:14*) He might as well have written: We know that we have passed from hell to heaven, because we love the breth-ren. He that loveth not his brother abideth in hell.

Finally, the heavenly life is centered in God Himself. God is all-in-all. It is the perfection of life under the Father's roof, with the Son's companionship, in the Spirit's power and holiness and vitality. When to St. John was granted his exalting vision of heaven, he de-scribed what he had seen in these words: "I saw no temple therein: for the Lord God Almighty and the Lamb are the temple of it." In other words, no religion in heaven! For the purpose of true religion in this life is to bring us *to* God, *toward* God; in heaven we shall have God.

"And the city had no need of the sun, neither of the moon, to shine in it: for the glory of God did lighten it, and the Lamb is the light thereof. And the nations of them which are saved shall walk in the light of it: and the kings of the earth do bring their glory and honour into it."

Everything in this present world which is truly glorious and honorable is gathered up into heaven and made perfect and eternal. Beethoven's music, Homer's poetry, Solon's statesmanship, Newton's science, Luther's courage, Francis of Assisi's saintliness, the ordinary mother's love for her child: all of these things which are the glory and honor of our life are triumphant and eternal in heaven. Nothing worth keeping is ever lost to the children of God. "And the gates of it shall not be shut at all by day: for there shall be no night there." (*Revelation 21:22-25*).

Such is the dear city of God which the faithful Christian sees by faith as the end of his journey and his eternal home. How does he know? By knowing God through Jesus Christ. This is all that he knows; but it is enough: for "this is life eternal, that they might know thee the only true God, and Jesus Christ, whom thou hast sent." (*St. John 17:3*)

Author's Notes

1. Paul Tillich, *The Courage to Be* (New Haven: Yale University Press, 1952), pp. 39-40. Quoted with permission.
2. I am indebted to *The Christian Faith* by Dr. C. B. Moss, for this summary of the New Testament data concerning the resurrection, and for very much else.
3. William Temple, *Readings in St. John's Gospel* (New York: St. Martin's Press, n.d.), pp. 384-85. Quoted with permission.
4. Hymn 587, *The Hymnal*, 1940.
5. These stanzas are from Hymns 584, 589, and 590 in *The Hymnal*, 1940.
6. Cyril Alington, *The Life Everlasting* (New York: Macmillan Co., n.d.), p. 68. Quoted with permission.
7. C. S. Lewis, *Screwtape Letters* (New York: Macmillan Co., n.d.), p. 64. Quoted with permission.
8. Harry N. Hancock, *And After This?* (New York: Longmans Green, 1954), p. 95. Quoted with permission.
9. I am unable to locate this passage among Bishop Gore's voluminous writings, but am certain that it is from his pen.

10. E. Towers, in *The Teaching of the Catholic Church* (New York: Macmillan Co., n.d.), I. 557. Quoted with permission.
11. William Temple, *Men's Creatrix* (New York: St. Martin's Press, n.d.), p. 349. Quoted with permission.
12. A. E. Taylor, *The Faith of a Moralist* (New York: St. Martin's Press, 1930), I. 387. Quoted with permission.
13. *Ibid.,* p. 408. Quoted with permission.